Do It Yourself

Treasure out of Trash

Do It Yourself

Treasure out of Trash

Author
Vinnie Mathur
Sunita Khanna

Illustrator/ Design
Himani Pundir

Graphic Designer
Bhupender Singh

Galgotia Publications pvt. ltd.

Edition 2008

Reprint 2010

ISBN:- 81-7515-585-X

Published by Suneel Galgotia for Galgotia Publications Pvt. Ltd.,
5, Ansari Road, Darya Ganj, New Delhi-110 002 and
printed at :- Tara Art Printers Pvt. Ltd.

Galgotia Publications pvt. ltd.

CONTENTS

Aquarium

Make your own aquarium at home and enjoy looking at the fish...

Things Required

- Acrylic paints
- Brushes
- Scissors
- Empty shoe box
- Blue cellophane paper
- Thread
- Tape

1

Take the shoe box and cut its bottom part, leaving 3 cms border all around.

2

Paint the box in light blue aqua colour and give it a sea effect.

3

Cut a piece of blue cellophane paper to fit inside the window and paste it with the help of tape.

4

Draw and colour fish of different shapes and also cut them out.

Beautiful Aquarium is ready.

5

Use tape to attach the thread to the fishes and tape the other end to the top of the box so that the fish look as if they are swimming.

Bangle Pen Stand

Use old bangles to make this lovely pen stand for your Teacher's desk…

Things Required

- 2 Thick bangles or kadas
- A dozen bangles
- Crafty glue
- A round juice tin or coke tin

Take an old juice tin and put glue all over it.

Place the big kada at the bottom of the tin and then put bangles on top of each other as shown.

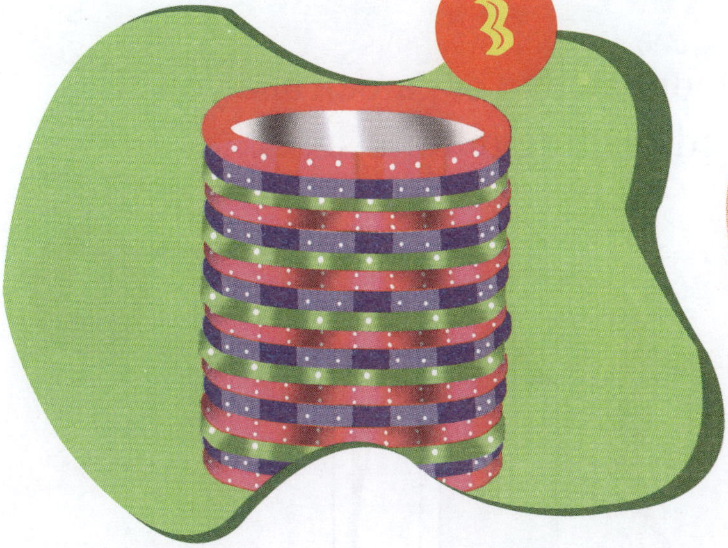

Repeat the same process up to the top as shown in the figure. You can use different coloured bangles to make it attractive and colourful.

Your colourful pen stand is ready to be gifted to your favourite teacher on Teacher's Day.

Bird Feeder

Hang this lovely feeder in your balcony or garden and you'll soon have a flock of birds calling in for a snack…

Things Required

- Empty rinsed out big juice carton
- Scissors
- Acrylic paints of brown, black and green colour
- Paint-brushes
- Bird seeds
- Net
- Wire

1

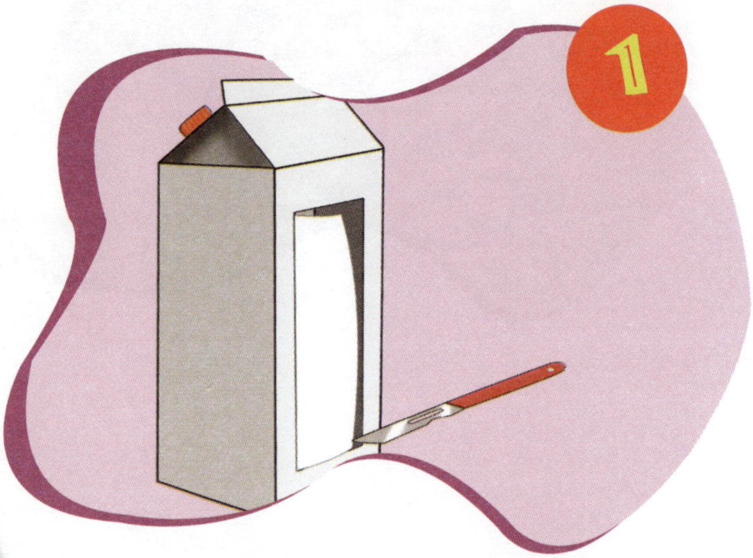

Take a juice carton and cut out a long window on the opposite side of the nozzle.

2

Paint the carton brown all over and leave it to dry.

Give a tree wood effect to the carton and add long streaks of brown, white and green to look like a bark.

Now draw leaves all over the carton with green paint.

Push a net bag full of seeds through the window and pull the top through the spout. Attach a wire to hang it.

Bird feeder is ready with snacks for birds.

Bottle Skittles

Make your own bowling alley at home with these skittles...

Things Required

- Paints of red, green and yellow colour
- 5 Old bottles
- Old jar
- Stickers
- Sparkles
- Funnel
- Sand
- Handwash

Take an old jar and also add a drop of hand-wash into it. Mix red paint with water until it looks like thin custard.

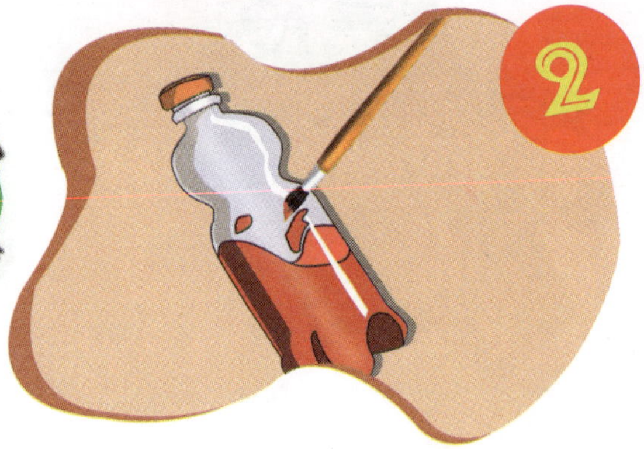

Pour some paint into the bottle, close its mouth with the top and shake it so that the paint spreads evenly inside. Then remove the top and let the paint dry.

Repeat the above steps for making other five bottles in different colours.

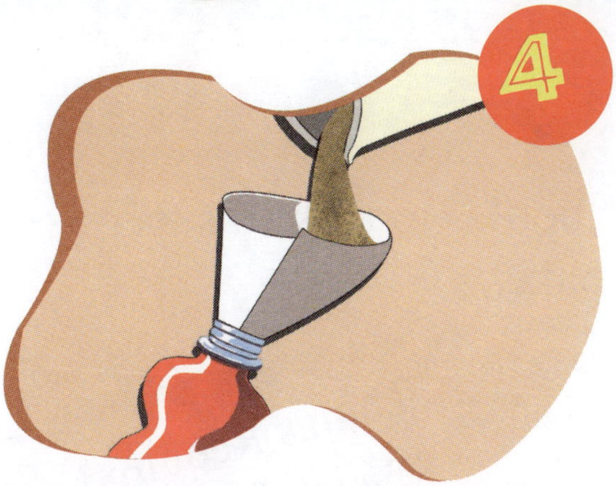

4

With the help of a funnel, put it inside the bottle and pour some sand into it covering halfway so that it makes the skittles harder to knock over. Repeat for each of the bottle.

5

Put the tops back on the bottles and decorate skittles all over with stars, sparkles and stickers.

Your bottle skittles are now ready.

Bottle-top Snake

Use the tops of fizzy water bottles to make a super slithery snake...

Paint the corks all over with green acrylic paint and leave them to dry.

Things Required

- 2 Wine corks
- Green acrylic paint and brush
- 18-20 Plastic bottle tops
- Old ball-point pen
- String
- 2 Googly eyes, small bell
- Scissors
- Pink paper
- Crafty glue

With Mummy's help ,make a hole in the middle of each bottle top, using an old ballpoint pen.

3

Screw one eye into the top of the wine cork. Add a bell to another screw eye, and screw this and the remaining eye into each end of the the cork.

4

Thread one end of the string through the bottom of a green bottle top. Now thread it through the cork eye and back through the bottle top. Make a knot and trim one end only.

5

Thread all the bottle tops on to the string, keeping them all the same way round. Finish by tying the string to the screw eye on the cork.

Glue the googly eyes or use bindis in place. Cut a pink strip of paper and paste it on to the cork for the snake's tongue.

Your bottle-top snake is now ready.

CD Clock

Time is very important for all of us. Let us learn to make a clock out of old CD lying at home...

Things Required

- An old CD
- A picture of your choice
- Crafty glue
- A watch machine
- Thin ribbon of any colour
- Two way tape

1

Take an old CD and cover one side with the picture of your choice with glue.

2

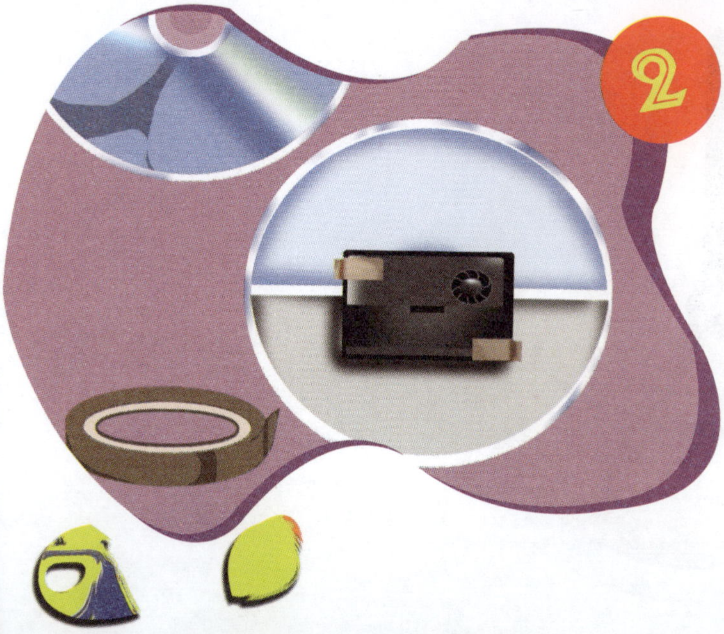

Take the machine, remove the hands, put the machine from the back and pierce from the centre of the CD. Stick the machine with the help of the two way tape.

Now put the hands of the CD on the front side.

For hanging the clock, make a loop starting from the head of the CD with any coloured ribbon.

Your CD clock is ready to tick-tock.

Cloth Bag

Make a beautiful cloth bag out of old dupatta or bed-cover lying at home…

Things Required

- Old dupatta
- Sparkles
- Fabric glue
- Scissors
- Paints and brushes
- Bindis, mirrors, feathers, old rakhis, laces, stars etc. for decoration

1

Cut dupatta in rectangle shape and join the two sides with fabric glue.

2

Cut two long strips of cloth for handle and paste them to on the top open side of the bag with fabric glue.

Now decorate the bag with sequins, stars or sparkles. You can also paint your bag.

Write a message like 'Say No To Plastic Bags' on your cloth bag.

Your cloth bag is ready to go for shopping.

Doll House

Make a small doll house for your pretty doll to stay in…

Things Required

- Empty cornflakes' box
- Crafty glue
- Scissors
- Red thick card
- Acrylic paints
- Brushes
- Old copy cover

Cut out the front part of the cornflakes' box, leaving it attached vertically to only one side of it.

Use an old copy cover to divide the box into half as shown in the picture.

Draw and cut three windows and a door on the box lid.

4

Cut a piece of red thick card of the same width as the box and twice the depth. Fold it into half. Cut out card triangles and glue them to each end to make the roof.

5

Paint around the windows and the door. Draw a money plant. Give the whole house a brick effect.

Your doll house is ready.

6

Decorate the bedroom and give pink colour to the walls.

Farmyard Barn

Save all your old cardboard boxes to make this great barn for your farmyard toys...

Things Required

- Any old cardboard box
- Scissors
- Brush and paints
- Crafty glue
- Green and pink paper
- Pencil and ruler
- Dry grass or straw

1

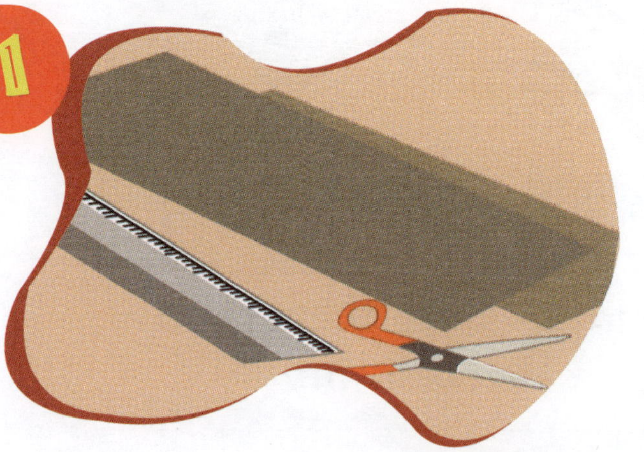

Cut two pieces of cardboard measuring 25 x 10 cm. These will be the base and back of the barn.

2

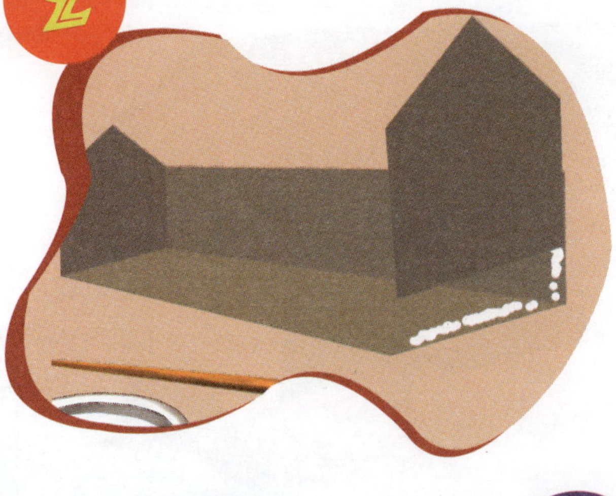

Now cut two more rectangles of 10 x 15 cm. Put them on top of one another and cut the corners off to make a roof shape.

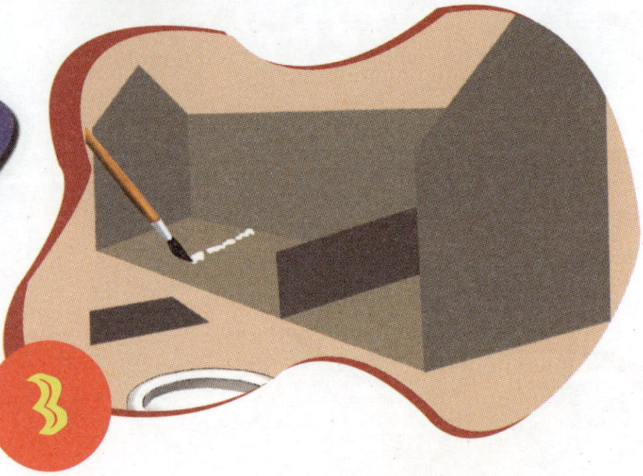

3

Cut three rectangles of 7 x 10 cm to make the stalls. Glue them and leave to dry.

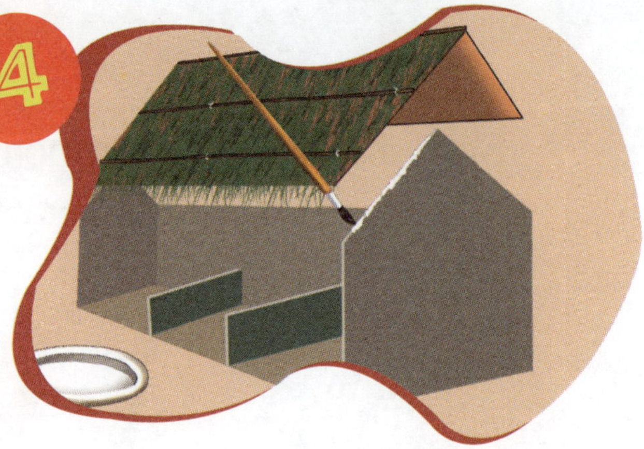

4

Cut a rectangle of 20 x 25 cm from the card. Make a crease by folding in half lengthways, then put it on top of the barn and glue it. Paint the barn in any colour of your choice.

5

Make a window on the side wall and put some grass and straw on the roof and the floor. When the paint has dried, decorate the barn.

Your farmyard barn is ready.

Foil Frame

Make this foil frame from old copy cover for your friends and relatives…

Things Required

- Old copy or diary cover
- Sparkles
- Scissors
- Crafty glue
- Sequins, beads etc.
- Pencil
- Kitchen foil

1

Take an old copy cover and draw two heart shapes of any size with a pencil. Cut it with scissors.

2

Take one heart shape and cut a square in the centre. Then cover it with kitchen foil as shown.

Glue the two hearts of card together, leaving a slot at the top. Slide a photo into the frame. Decorate the front side with coloured sequins and beads.

Make a loop out of ribbon and paste at the back side of the frame to hang.

Your foil frame is ready to gift.

Key Holder

Reuse ice cream sticks and make this lovely key holder..

Things Required

- Ice-cream sticks
- Crafty glue
- Acrylic colours
- Brush
- Old wedding card
- Key hooks

Draw any shape like a hut on the back side of the thick wedding card and cut it out.

Stick ice-cream sticks next to each other to cover the card.

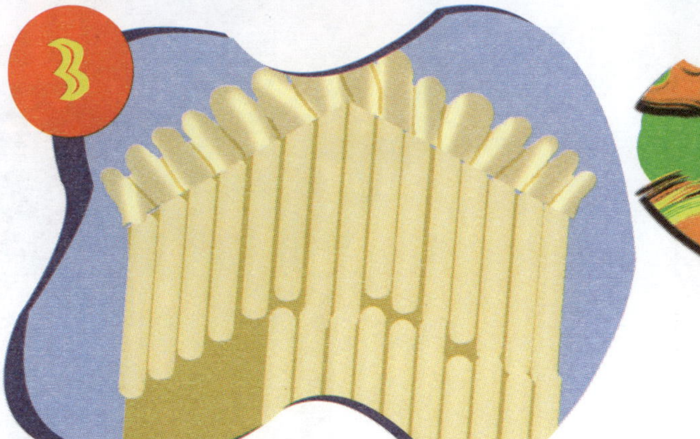

Make the roof separately as shown in the picture and stick it to the body of the house.

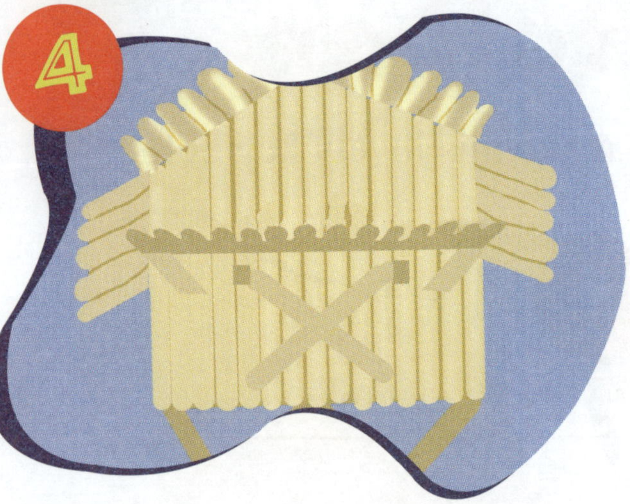

Paste sticks over each other at the base of the house to put the key hooks.

Paint the house using acrylic colours of your choice and leave it to dry for a day.

Hang this key holder in your room now !!

Magazine Holder

Make this magazine holder from old dupatta or saree…

Things Required

- Old dupatta
- Metal ring or bangle
- Sparkles, old mirrors
- Ribbon
- Scissors
- Crafty glue
- Rubber band

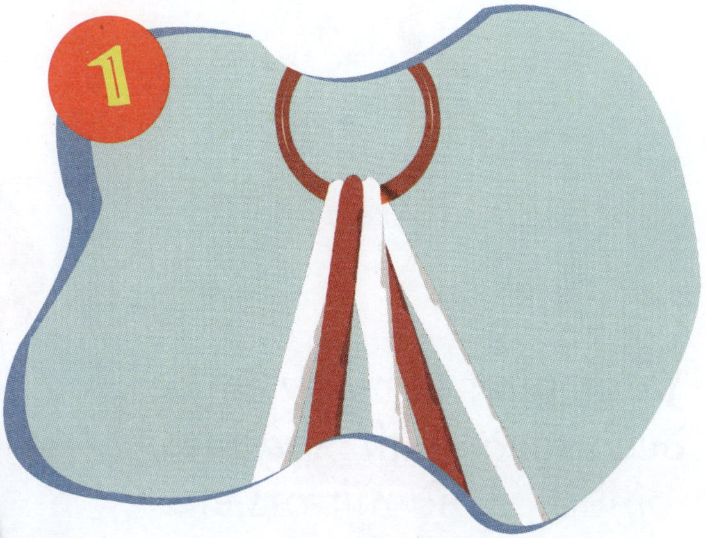

Cut three long and equal strips from old dupatta and insert them into a metal ring or bangle as shown above.

Make a tight plait, like the one we make for our hair.

Make 12 folds and after every 4 folds, tie a rubber band and a ribbon.

Your plait is ready to be decorated with sparkles, bindis or old mirrors etc.

In between the folds, you can put the newspapers or magazines.

Mini Shell Box

Reuse mummy's old jewellery box to make this decorative mini box...

Things required

- Small old jewellery box
- Scissors, crafty glue
- Assorted seashells
- Sparkle
- Old dupatta or wrapping paper

1

Take an old jewellery box and empty it.

2

Cover it with wrapping paper or old dupatta.

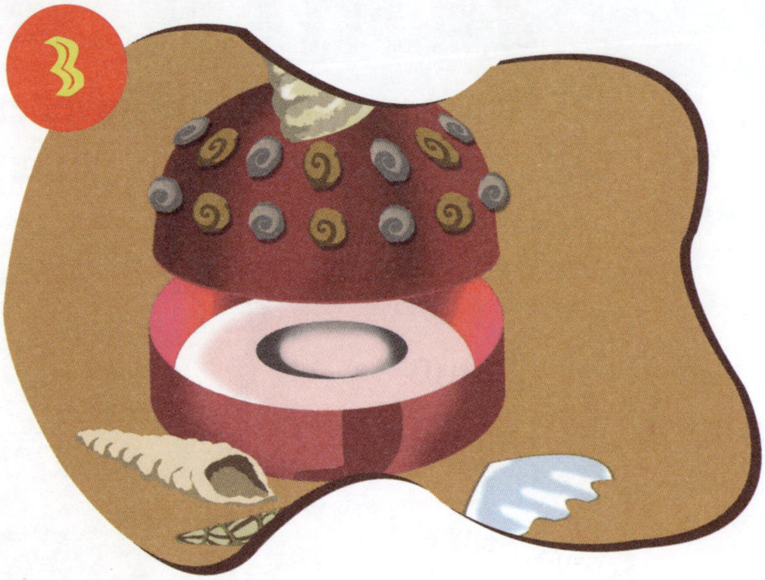

Arrange the shells in a decorative manner on the top of the box and glue them. Use sparkles to further enhance the decoration of the box.

Now your lovely shell box is ready.

Mobile Pouch

Make this lovely mobile pouch out of an ordinary piece of cloth...

Things required

- Old piece of cloth
- Ribbon
- Scissors
- Golden lace
- Needle and thread

Take an old dupatta or any ordinary cloth and cut it into two rectangular pieces.

Sew the two pieces together with needle and thread leaving top side open.

3

Take a strip of ribbon or thread and sew it also to the top ends of the holder to make a handle.

4

Decorate the sides of the pouch with golden lace or ribbon.

Your mobile pouch is ready to use.

Teddy Mirror

Mirror mirror on the wall, oops doll ! Now you can look at your two favourite people at the same time; you and your pet doll or any toy or teddy…

Things Required

- Cardboard out of old copy cover
- Drawing of a doll or teddy
- Poster colours
- Crafty glue, scissors
- A small round mirror
- Ribbon, an old bangle
- Sparkles

Make drawing of a doll or a teddy and paint it with colourful poster colours. Leave it to dry.

When dried, cut out the edges.

Paste the picture on to your copy cover. Then draw the outline and cut that too.

Place the mirror in the centre of the teddy and decorate further with sparkles. Attach a bangle at the back of the teddy for it to hang on the wall.

Your cute little mirror is ready.

Wooden Hanger

Make your room and bathroom neat and tidy by making a wooden hanger out of some left over wooden pieces...

Things Required

- A rectangular piece of wooden board
- 3 Enamel paints of your choice
- A metallic hook for the back
- Hooks for hanging clothes

1

Take a rectangular piece of wood. Paint it beautifully.

2

Fix a hook at the back of it for hanging.

3

Now fix two or three hooks according to the size of your wooden hanger in the centre or at the bottom of the frame.

Your beautiful hanger is ready for use. Make more for gifting to your near and dear ones.